RIVER
ADVENTURES

YANGTZE

W
FRANKLIN WATTS
LONDON•SYDNEY

First published 2012 by Franklin Watts
Hachette Children's Books
338 Euston Road
London NW1 3BH

Franklin Watts Australia
Level 17/207 Kent Street
Sydney, NSW 2000

Designed, edited and produced by Paul Manning
Maps by Stefan Chabluk
Proofread and indexed by Alice Harman

Produced for Franklin Watts by
White-Thomson Publishing Ltd

www.wtpub.co.uk
+44 (0) 845 208 7460

A CIP catalogue record for this book is available
from the British Library.

ISBN 978 0 7496 1038 7

Dewey classification: 915.1'2

Printed in China

Franklin Watts is a division of
Hachette Children's Books,
an Hachette UK company
www.hachette.co.uk

Key to images

Top cover image: Pudong district, Shanghai
Main cover image: Cormorant fishing on the Yangtze
Previous page: Cormorant with alligator gar fish
This page: The Three Gorges Dam, Hubei province,
China.

Note to Teachers and Parents

Every effort has been made to ensure that the websites
listed on page 32 are suitable for children, that they are
of the highest educational value and that they contain
no inappropriate or offensive material. However,
because of the nature of the Internet, it is impossible
to guarantee that the content of these sites will not be
altered. We strongly recommend that Internet access is
supervised by a responsible adult.

Picture Credits

Front cover t, Shutterstock/aspen rock; front cover main, Shutterstock/aspen rock;
1, Dreamstime/Jose Garcia; 2-3, Dreamstime/Aschwin Prein; 4, Shutterstock/
Stephen Rudolph; 5t (map), Stefan Chabluk; 5b, NPL/Mark Carwardine; 6,
Shutterstock/Lukas Hlavac; 7t, Shutterstock/Jun Mu; 7b, Corbis/Ye Erjiang; 8,
Wikimedia/Gisling; 9t, Dreamstime/Javarman; 9b, Wikimedia/Brücke-Osteuropa;
10, courtesy International Rivers; 11, Wikimedia/Corto Maltese; 12-13,
Wikimedia/Oliver Ren; 13t, Dreamstime/86ccyy; 14, Wikimedia/Leberhard; 15t,
Getty/Tim Graham; 15b, Dreamstime/Aschwin Prein; 16, Dreamstime/Jjspring;
17t, Wikimedia/Yu Hui; 17b, Wikimedia/Remi Jouan; 18, Dreamstime/Kun Yang;
19t, Dreamstime/Aschwin Prein; 19b, Getty/STR; 20, Wikimedia/neurozee; 21t,
Wikimedia/Yu Hui; 21b, Dreamstime/Chuyu; 22, Dreamstime/Mark Amy; 23t,
Dreamstime/Lee Snider; 23b, Wikimedia/Wuzhen Xizha; 24, Dreamstime/Xi Zhang;
25t, Wikimedia/Farm; 25b, Wikimedia/Tomtom08; 26, Getty/ChinaFotoPress; 27t,
Wikimedia/Max W; 27b, Dreamstime/Beetle2k42; 28, Dreamstime/Jacklee1986; 29,
Wikimedia/Marqueed; 31a, Wikimedia/Sitomon; 31b, Wikimedia/T.Voekler; 31c,
Dreamstime/Mike Hollman; 31d, Dreamstime/Paulhenk; 31f, Wikimedia/
Ondrej Žváček; 31g, Wikimedia/www.voithsiemens.com.

CONTENTS

A Yangtze Journey

The Yangtze is Asia's longest river, stretching for 6,300 km (3,915 miles). Its Chinese name is 'Chang Jiang', which means 'the Long River'. You will follow the river from its source on the Qinghai–Tibet Plateau to where it drains into the East China Sea near Shanghai.

A great river

Chinese civilization began on the banks of the Yangtze. For thousands of years, Chinese people have relied on the river for transport, for irrigating crops and for food and water. Today, about half of all the food in China is grown in the Yangtze basin, including more than two-thirds of the country's rice crop. Almost 500 million people live and work along its banks.

▼ As well as farmed hillsides like this, the Yangtze flows through many different landscapes, including mountains, forests, fertile plains and wetlands.

Threats to the Yangtze

In recent years, the river has become badly polluted by factory and household waste. Wildlife habitats have been destroyed, and many types of fish that once lived in the river have disappeared. The Chinese government is working to repair the damage and to protect endangered species. Some sections of the river have now been made into nature reserves.

The Yangtze's source

Finding the source of a river like the Yangtze is not easy because many other streams, called tributaries, flow into it. People once thought that the Jinsha Jiang River was the source. Then, in 1976, a small lake was discovered at the foot of Mount Geladandong near the border with Tibet. Most now agree that this lake is the Yangtze's source.

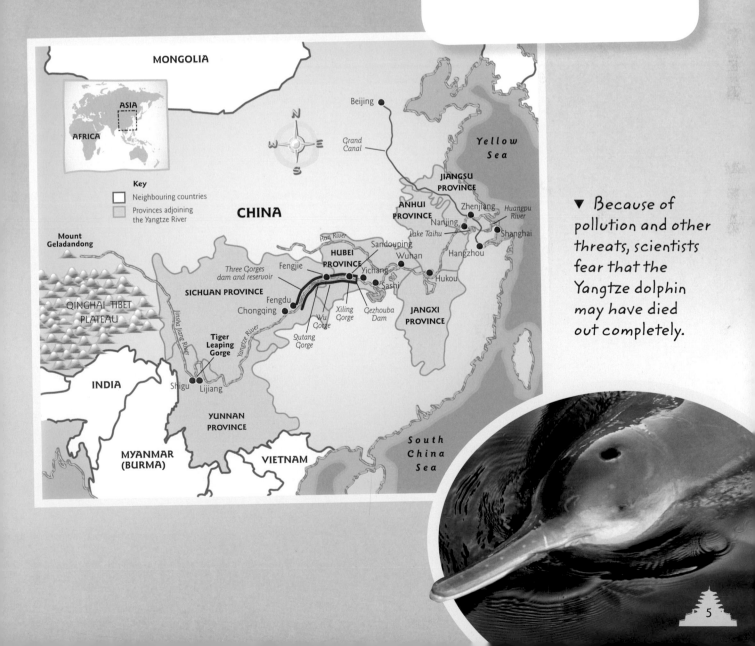

MONGOLIA

ASIA

AFRICA

Beijing

Grand Canal

Yellow Sea

Key
Neighbouring countries
Provinces adjoining the Yangtze River

CHINA

JIANGSU PROVINCE

ANHUI PROVINCE

Zhenjiang   *Huangpu River*

Nanjing

Lake Taihu   Shanghai

Mount Geladandong

Hou River

Sandouping

HUBEI PROVINCE

Wuhan

Hangzhou

Three Gorges dam and reservoir   Fengjie

Yichang

Hukou

SICHUAN PROVINCE

Fengdu   Sashi

QINGHAI–TIBET PLATEAU

Chongqing

Wu Gorge   *Xiling Gorge*   *Gezhouba Dam*

JANGXI PROVINCE

Jinsha Jiang River

Yangtze River   *Qutang Gorge*

Tiger Leaping Gorge

INDIA

Shigu   Lijiang

YUNNAN PROVINCE

South China Sea

MYANMAR (BURMA)   **VIETNAM**

▼ *Because of pollution and other threats, scientists fear that the Yangtze dolphin may have died out completely.*

5

The Tibetan Plateau

CHINA
Mt. Geladandong
Qinghai–Tibet Plateau
SICHUAN
Yangtze River
Shigu
YUNNAN

YOU ARE HERE

The Yangtze's source, Mount Geladandong, is high on the Qinghai–Tibet Plateau in western China. As you fly over the plateau, you can see how vast and remote this region is.

▼ *The Tibetan Plateau is sometimes called the 'roof of the world'. It is four times the size of France. Many of the great rivers of Asia begin here.*

The Upper Yangtze

The Yangtze starts by flowing east through a shallow valley. It then winds south past snow-covered mountain peaks that are cut with steep rocky valleys called gorges. On flat parts of the plateau, nomadic tribesmen live by herding cattle. They do not have a permanent home, but move from place to place, living in circular tents called yurts.

▼ The first turn of the Yangtze at Shigu in Yunnan Province, where the river heads northeast.

The Yangtze's 'first turn'

For several hundred kilometres, the Yangtze flows southeast. Then, at a small town called Shigu, it meets a massive wall of limestone and turns suddenly northeast. This is known as the 'first turn' of the Yangtze.

Until fifty years ago, this part of China was cut off from the rest of the world. Its people lived under their own rulers. Today, roads and railways are being built, and the way of life here is changing. But many areas are still very remote. Some villages are so isolated they can only be reached by mountain paths and rope bridges.

The Kazak people

The mountains of northwestern China are home to around 800,000 nomadic Kazak people. In the summer, they set up their homes high in the mountains, where there are pastures for their cattle. When autumn comes, they move lower down, packing up their tents and taking their belongings with them.

▶ A Kazak family leave the plains in search of fresh pastures.

Tiger Leaping Gorge

YOU ARE HERE

SICHUAN
Yangtze River
Tiger Leaping Gorge
Lijiang
YUNNAN

At Lijiang, roughly 20 km (12 miles) east of Shigu, you catch a bus to Tiger Leaping Gorge. Over millions of years, this dramatic gorge has been carved out of the rock by the fast-flowing Yangtze River.

▼ Tiger Leaping Gorge is one of the world's deepest gorges. Its name comes from a local legend in which a tiger escaped from a hunter by leaping across the river.

At Tiger Leaping Gorge, the Yangtze falls 300 m (984 ft) over a series of 18 rapids. Below the viewing point where you are standing now, the river hurtles through a gap just 30 m (100 ft) wide. The roar of the water echoes off sheer rock walls, which tower up to 3,000 m (9,850 ft) high on either side of you.

▲ The ancient city of Lijiang was once an important trading and cultural centre. Today, its income comes mainly from tourism.

The Naxi

Returning to Lijiang, you explore the old part of the city, with its narrow cobbled streets and traditional wooden houses.

The people of this area, called the Naxi, have a rich history. They originally came from Tibet, but settled here more than a thousand years ago. In the past, the Naxi lived by farming and herding. Since tourists started to visit Lijiang, many Naxi people now earn a living by making goods to sell in local shops.

▶ Naxi people follow an ancient religion called Dongba. They worship the natural world around them, including the sun, moon, mountains and rivers.

The Lijiang earthquake

In 1996, a major earthquake struck the Lijiang region. About a third of the city was destroyed, including many of its oldest buildings. Afterwards, Lijiang was rebuilt and developed as a centre for tourism. Many people now come to visit the region and to learn about the culture of the Naxi people.

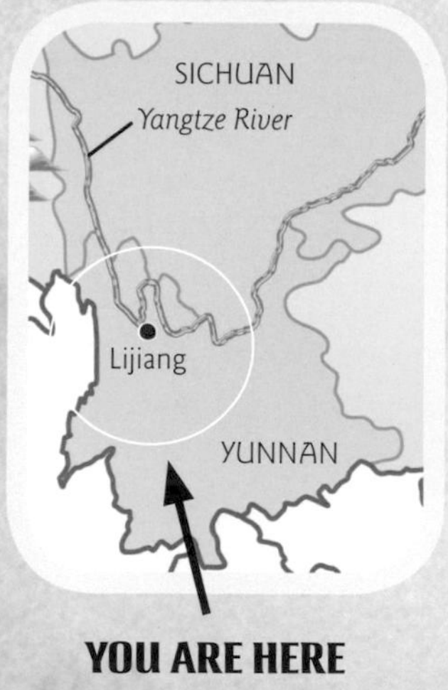

YOU ARE HERE

SICHUAN
Yangtze River

Lijiang

YUNNAN

Farming the Valleys

In the mountains around Lijiang, farmers have cut steps into the hillsides to create level strips of land called terraces. These are used for growing crops.

Terracing

Stone walls help to support the terraces and hold the soil in place. The farmers also cut ditches to carry water from nearby streams to their fields. Much of the farm work is done by hand, but water buffalo are used to plough the fields before planting.

▼ On steep hillside plots, ploughing with buffalo or oxen is easier than using a tractor.

Erosion

Spring and summer are the rainy season in the Upper Yangtze, and there are often heavy storms. When it rains, water pours down the slopes, washing away crops and soil. This causes the land to be eroded.

When too many trees are cut down or animals are allowed to overgraze the land, erosion can be a big problem. Since the 1950s, many forests along the Yangtze have been cut down for timber or firewood. Without the trees to hold the land together, soil is washed into the river. This makes the channel shallow and muddy and increases the danger of flooding.

Deforestation

Land in the Yangtze basin has been badly damaged by deforestation. After disastrous floods in 1998, the Chinese government decided it was time to act. Laws were passed to prevent tree-cutting and overgrazing. Local people were told about the dangers of cutting down trees, and new trees were planted in deforested areas.

Chongqing

SICHUAN

Chongqing

Yangtze River

Lijiang

YUNNAN

YOU ARE HERE

At Chongqing, you reach the first big city on your journey. This great trading and industrial centre began as a riverside port. It is now the biggest city in China, and one of the fastest-growing cities in the world.

▼ *Industrial fumes pollute the air over Chongqing, the biggest inland river port in western China.*

The Yangtze has been vital to the growth of Chongqing. From the city's docks, millions of tonnes of cargo are transported along the river every day. Since the building of the Three Gorges Dam, big ships can now travel here all the way from the East China Sea.

▶ Factories in Chongqing produce everything from textiles to electrical goods. Nearly all the goods produced here are transported out of the city by river.

Industrial growth

The old city of Chongqing dates back to the 4th century. Built on the clifftops and flanked by the river to the west, it was a natural fortress and easy to defend.

In the 1970s, the Chinese government chose Chongqing as a centre of industrial growth, and many new factories were built here. Since then, it has expanded at an amazing rate. Around 30 million people now live in the Chongqing region, and half a million more arrive every year.

A veil of fog

During the spring and autumn, a thick layer of fog covers Chongqing. In recent years, smoke and pollution from factories has made the problem worse, and a haze of fumes called smog hangs in the air. The poor air quality is bad for people's health. The city's government is now trying to reduce the pollution.

The Flooded Valley

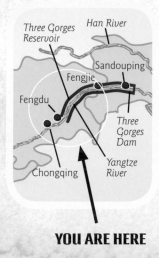

YOU ARE HERE

At Chongqing, you board a passenger boat for the next leg of your journey. This part of the river has been transformed by the building of the Three Gorges Dam downstream.

Drowned cities

When the dam was built, the entire river valley between Chongqing and Sandouping was flooded. This now forms a reservoir 640 km (397 miles) long. Thirteen cities were rebuilt higher up the river banks, and thousands of hectares of farmland disappeared underwater. The flooding of the valley has changed this part of China forever.

▼ Since the flooding of the river valley, the Yangtze carries more traffic than ever. This carrier is transporting a cargo of trucks from a factory in Chongqing.

◀ This new town was built to rehouse people who lost their homes because of the Three Gorges Dam.

More than a million people were ordered to leave their homes to make way for the dam. Although they were given money by the government, many did not want to leave the homes where they had lived for generations.

River traffic

Since the valley was flooded, the river has risen by as much as 175 m (570 ft). This has opened the way for many more ships to use the river. In the past, sand and gravel on the riverbed were a danger to shipping. Now ocean-going ships can travel the river safely. This extra traffic has brought great wealth to Chongqing and other cities further downriver.

The 'Ghost City' of Fengdu

Dating back 1,800 years, the 'Ghost City' of Fengdu was an ancient burial site that was famous throughout China for its statues of demons and devils. Since the flooding of the river valley, much of the city is now underwater and most of the original shrines have been lost.

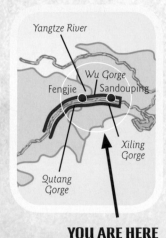

YOU ARE HERE

The Three Gorges

At Fengjie, you board a cruise boat to explore the Three Gorges. These spectacular limestone gorges stretch for 130 km (80 miles). They are among the most famous sights in China.

▼ River cruises on the Yangtze are a growing source of income for the Three Gorges region.

Qutang Gorge, the first of the three gorges, is the shortest and narrowest. The mountains on either side are 1,200 m (3,900 ft) high, and tower over the river. Along the sides of the gorge you can still see ancient pathways carved into the rock, where teams of men used to haul boats upstream.

◀ The point where the river passes between these mountains is called the Kuimen Gate. It marks the entrance to Qutang Gorge.

The Yangtze Gorges

Experts believe that the Yangtze River first began to cut a path through the mountains around 45 million years ago. The transport route formed by the river has been vital to China ever since. Without it, the fertile Sichuan Province, 'China's rice bowl', would have been almost completely cut off from the rest of the country.

In **Wu Gorge** an ancient legend tells how 12 wild dragons who brought chaos and floods to the land were defeated by Yao Ji, daughter of the Queen Mother of the West. After her death, Yao Ji and her sisters were turned into 12 great mountain peaks – six on either side of the gorge.

The third gorge, **Xiling**, is 76 km (47 miles) long. In the past, travellers often drowned in the powerful whirlpools and rapids here. Since the river valley was flooded, Xiling has become less dangerous, but boats still keep between markers that show the safest route.

▶ People have been travelling the Yangtze in boats since ancient times. This traditional type of sailing boat is called a junk.

Han River
Three Gorges Dam
Sandouping
Xiling Gorge
Yangtze River

YOU ARE HERE

Three Gorges Dam

As you leave Xiling Gorge, you come face to face with one of the great wonders of modern China – the huge Three Gorges Dam.

An engineering triumph

The dam is a great achievement for China. For centuries, floods along the Yangtze brought terrible suffering to the Chinese people. The dam controls the flow of the river and reduces the risk of flooding. It is also the world's largest hydroelectric plant, producing vital energy for China's fast-growing towns and cities.

▼ As well as reducing the risk of flooding, the giant Three Gorges Dam supplies 10 per cent of China's energy needs.

◄ This huge lock allows ships and cargo boats to bypass the Three Gorges Dam and carry on their journey along the river.

The impact of the dam

Since it was completed in 2009, the Three Gorges Dam has brought prosperity to many parts of China – but not all its effects have been good.

As well as forcing people to leave their homes, it has harmed wildlife and the environment. Rubbish and pollution have built up in the dam reservoir, and fish have been poisoned. Water from the dam reservoir has eroded the hillsides, and many parts of the river valley have been affected by landslides. Some experts believe that the weight of water in the reservoir may even be damaging the Earth's crust.

The Yangtze floods

In the last century, thousands died as a result of flooding on the Yangtze. In 1998 the floods were among the worst ever, destroying homes, devastating crops and livestock and leaving thousands dead or homeless. Despite the building of the Three Gorges Dam, flooding caused by heavy monsoon rains still affects many areas of the country.

▶ People rescue belongings during floods on the Yangtze in 2010.

Han
River
Wuhan
Yichang
Yangtze
River
Sashi

YOU ARE HERE

Yichang to Wuhan

At Yichang, you leave the mountains and gorges behind. The river flows more slowly here, broadening out across flat, low-lying land. This is the start of the Yangtze's great flood plain.

Industrial cities

▼ A cargo boat brings supplies of building materials to the city of Yichang.

As well as farming, there is industry on this part of the river. Electricity from the nearby Gezhouba Dam has turned Yichang into a fast-growing industrial city. About 150 km (93 miles) downstream, Shashi is another booming industrial town, with cotton mills, dyeworks and machinery plants.

◄ The 1957 Wuhan Yangtze Bridge was the first ever built across the Yangtze.

China tea

In the 19th century, Hankou was a centre of the tea trade. Ships from Great Britain sailed up the river to collect their cargo, then raced for home. Tea spoils if it is kept too long at sea, so the fastest ships fetched the best prices. On one voyage, the famous Cutty Sark covered a record 584 km (362 miles) in a single day.

Wuhan

The most important city in this region is Wuhan. Here, the Yangtze is joined by its longest tributary, the Han River.

Wuhan's main industry is iron and steel-making. The city dates back nearly 2,000 years. Three cities – Hankou, Hanyang and Wuchang – grew up around the meeting of the rivers, before eventually merging into one. It was not until 1957 that they were linked by a bridge across the Yangtze.

▶ Wuhan's Yellow Crane Tower is a famous landmark overlooking the river.

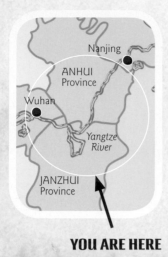

YOU ARE HERE

The Lower Yangtze

Beyond the city of Wuhan, you enter the 'land of fish and rice'. This fertile region produces around 70 per cent of China's paddy rice and more than half of its freshwater fish.

Rice growing

Rice is China's single most important food. Most of it is grown in fields called paddies by the river. Rice plants need lots of water to grow. Some of the water comes from rain, but most is pumped from the river and piped to the nearby fields.

Once the rice has been picked, it is threshed to separate the waste from the grain, then stored. Finally, the field is ploughed, ready for a new crop to be planted.

▼ These flooded paddy fields need to be supplied with water all the year round.

◀ Planting rice by hand is hard work in the hot sun.

Yangtze silt

When the Yangtze floods, it brings with it a rich layer of sediment called silt that helps to nourish the soil and make it fertile. Since the building of the Three Gorges Dam, the river brings less silt. This is because much of the sediment gets trapped in the huge reservoir behind the dam.

Fish from the river

The Yangtze has always been a rich source of fish, including carp, bream, perch and sturgeon. There are thousands of lakes around Wuhan, and fishing and fish-farming are vital industries. Because of pollution and overfishing, the number of fish has fallen recently. In some areas, fishing is now banned altogether during the breeding season, so that fish stocks have a chance to recover.

▶ This fisherman has birds called cormorants, which he has trained to help him catch fish in the river.

YOU ARE HERE

Nanjing

From Hukou, the Yangtze gently descends through plains, hills, lakes and wetland before reaching the ancient city of Nanjing.

City walls

As you enter the outskirts of Nanjing, the city's stone walls come into view. In earlier times, these high walls protected the people of the city from attack. Nowadays, the buildings of the old city are surrounded by high-rise blocks and modern shopping and business districts.

▼ Old and new buildings line the river in the centre of Nanjing.

► Nanjing's stone walls stretch for 32 km (20 miles) around the city.

Nanjing was once the capital of China, and has often played an important part in the country's history. It is also a key commercial and industrial centre, and many transport routes meet here.

The Grand Canal

About 80 km (50 miles) beyond Nanjing, you meet another important waterway. The Grand Canal runs between Beijing in the north and Hangzhou in the south, crossing the Yangtze at Zhenjiang. Stretching for 1,800 km (1,118 miles), the Grand Canal is the longest man-made waterway in the world.

▼ In places, the Grand Canal is so busy that extra channels have been built around major cities to reduce the traffic jams.

A vital waterway

The Grand Canal was completed nearly 2,000 years ago to allow farmers in southern China to transport grain to the northern cities. Nearly 6 million labourers helped to build it, and many died during its construction. Today, it is a vital route for barges carrying building materials to the rapidly developing delta area.

YOU ARE HERE

The Yangtze Delta

Below Nanjing, the Yangtze is tidal. This means that its flow is affected by the twice-daily rise and fall of the tides in the East China Sea.

▼ Lake Taihu in the Yangtze Delta is the third-largest freshwater lake in China. These workers are clearing green algae caused by sewage pollution.

Draining the Delta

As the river approaches the sea, the incoming tide slows its movement. Silt is dropped to form a maze of marshy islands, sandbanks and water channels. This is known as the river delta.

A hundred years ago, the Yangtze Delta was mostly swamp. Since then, many of the marshes have been drained and the river banks raised to protect against flooding. Today, the delta is one of the most crowded places on Earth, with a population of more than 80 million.

◀ This new road bridge is part of a 25-km (15-mile) bridge and tunnel network connecting Shanghai with Chongming Island in the north.

Flood protection

Along the Yangtze are roughly 1,700 km (1,050 miles) of flood barriers, many dating back to ancient times. One of the oldest is the Zhenjiang levée. This 182 km (113 mile) dyke protects 8 million people, two major cities and 800,000 hectares (3,100 sq miles) of farmland.

A dynamic region

As China's economy has grown, the Yangtze Delta has become heavily developed. To reduce overcrowding in the main city of Shanghai, more than a million people were moved out to ten new settlements in the Delta. Each of these new towns has its own industrial zone, mostly specialising in growth industries such as ICT and electronics.

Meanwhile, in Shanghai itself, a huge scheme was launched to rebuild the city's water supply system and reduce pollution. You will see the amazing growth of Shanghai as you reach the last stage of your journey.

▼ Siberian crane are among many migrating birds that spend the winter in the Yangtze Delta.

Websites and Further Reading

Websites

- www.kids.nationalgeographic.com/kids/
  places/find/china
  Good short introduction to China.
- www.worldwildlife.org/what/
  wherewework/yangtze/index.html
  Useful information on Yangtze wildlife.
- www.wwf.org.uk/what_we_do/
  safeguarding_the_natural_world/rivers_
  and_lakes/where_we_work/yangtze_
  china.cfm
  Interesting material on environmental
  issues facing the Yangtze wetlands.

Further reading

The Yangtze (Rivers of Life series),
Michael Pollard (Evans, 2010)

The Yangtze (Journey Along a River series),
Jen Green (Wayland, 2009)

*The Yangtze: China's Majestic River
(Rivers Around the World* series),
Molly Aloian (Crabtree, 2010)

Index

Answers to Yangtze Quiz

1 1B, 2C, 3A, 4F, 5D, 6E. **2** Shanghai, Wuhan, Fengjie,
Chongqing, Lijiang, Shigu. **3** All four are man-made or natural
features of Qutang Gorge, the shortest of the Three Gorges.
4 One of the giant turbines of the Three Gorges Dam. Water from
the dam drives the turbine, which generates hydroelectricity.